Black Lives Matter and Other Poems

Poems by Joseph Anthony Davis

Kansas City Spartan Press Missouri

Spartan Press
Kansas City, Missouri
spartanpresskc.com

Copyright (c) Joseph Davis, 2018
First Edition 1 3 5 7 9 10 8 6 4 2
ISBN: 978-1-946642-41-7
LCCN: 2018931382

Design, edits and layout: Jason Ryberg
Author photo: Hayley E. Zahnter
Cover photo: Jon Bidwell
All rights reserved. No part of this publication may be reproduced or transmitted in any form or by any means, electronic or mechanical, including photocopying, recording or by info retrieval system, without prior written permission from the author.

ACKNOWLEDGMENTS

Spartan Press would like to thank Prospero's Books, The Fellowship of N-finite Jest, The Prospero Institute of Disquieted P/o/e/t/i/c/s, Will Leathem, Tom Wayne, Jeanette Powers, j.d.tulloch, Jon Bidwell, Jason Preu, Mark McClane, Tony Hayden and the whole Osage Arts Community.

Thank you to Hayley E. Zahnter for the author photo and to the proofreading and editing perseverance and patience of Jason (insert your middle intital here - optional, of course) Ryberg. THOU ROCKEST, sir.

CONTENTS

The Poet Bids Farewell to All Notions
   of Moving to Seattle / 1
When This Poetry Deal Goes Down / 3
Summer Notes / 4
Palimpsest / 6
Festival Kite in Night Sky / 7
Watching TV with Grandma / 11
A Murder in Volker Park (Springtime
   Horror) / 12
Along Highway 45 towards Atchison, Kansas / 13
The Cleansing / 15
Summer Magic / 16
Semester's End / 18
john wayne in the ghetto / 20
The Prodigal Nerd Returns / 22
Dancing Alone at the Edge of the Universe / 26
Thinking about the Female Shapeshifter in
   STAR TREK: DEEP SPACE NINE (or, Your
   Amerikkkan Fetish) / 28
Sonata in C: One Drunk's Response to this
   Post-9/11 World: Supplication and Dedication / 31
Consumption / 33
Catastrophes and Conflagrations / 40
Closure / 48

Smirk / 50

Black Lives Matter / 52

Thoughts in a Dark Alley / 56

The Belly of a Single Tear / 57

soft, boyish hands / 58

Ode of Calm Release / 59

Janice Elizabeth Davis and John Henry Davis III, you are the best evidence of the great love between our mother and father, the late, great Jean Louise Jefferies Davis and John Henry Davis, Jr.; continue to thrive and heal. Jeanne Kliewer, I am certain you are a superb sister-in-law.

To all my friends and family, by blood or by choice, who believed in me when I chose not to believe in myself.

To All Souls Unitarian Universalist Church, thank you for the space, camaraderie, music and fellowship to own my humanism, and finally, all my love and light to the family that is It's A Beautiful Day, and to Barry Morse and Brent Canter — thank you.

The Poet Bids Farewell to All Notions
of Moving to Seattle

Bid farewell to that pretension of leaving for that
salubrious and progressive place because you know
there are no panaceas or other quick fixes there or here.
Bid farewell to the clamor and bling of that emerald
metropolis that people mention with begrudging
admiration as though it was El Dorado or Fatima with
its fictitious, dancing sun. You can always visit, but it was
never home. You blindsided your way back home to
Kansas City. Caught up in the well-wishes and good
wedding cheer of family and friends who suffered your
alcoholic flights of fancy, your repressed and distressed
sexuality; you reveled in the newness of the light rail, and
the pageantry of a summer day on Puget Sound that
stimulated your poetic senses, giving way to diminishing
sparkle of sunset, as the coffeehouses close and the Capitol
Hill bohemia turns into a night gallery of homeless youth,
furtive cruising and the insomniac's walking meditation.

Bid farewell to all fantasy you attached to that place: that
it could deaden the ache, close the breach and somehow
still be made authentic and incorruptible. You are a poet,
a writer, and as such, a marauder of all pretension and
delusion. You may trifle with music and possess a singing
voice good enough for the Unitarian choir but anyone
who knows you KNOWS you love to make words clash
and asonate and consonate together with a child's
delirious joy of saying something with that clarity that
makes his parents proud.

Whatever pageantry and pretensions of liberation you felt when you walked the rhythms of that elusive, emerald city, discover and uncover the relief in the avoidance of being another posing transplant, that 12% unemployment line, and the flagellating utterances of an aunt's unsettling addiction to Jesus, presence is right here with you in the 816 and 641; you have earned the right to love it here. You persist in exorcising ghosts in this city of your birth and rebirth and rebirth yet again, and it is succeeding, and this tall, black skin you're in fits you perfectly.

In its eternal spinning conspiracy with earth of gentle reprove and plaintive warmth, sunrise, in its conspiracy with the spinning earth, bathes you as you work this job you don't understand, and the reason you enjoy it so much—cleaning up along Broadway ... from 36th Street to the Corner Restaurant and the Westport library, even after the homeless poop in alcoves or scatter their hoarded, meager belongings in Millcreek Park. The brow furrows and the sweat finds the surface of air and skin and in that toil, you know you will not go crazy ... writing, at least.

But in the event you do, assure that last sane soul who sees you that it was not under the enchanting delusion of a life in the mega-music business, a stifling Christianity that haunts too close to skin and kin, or reading too much Daniel Quinn. Conjuring up unearned accolades with cavalcades of acolytes genuflecting at every churlish trope you may belch up from the insulating dregs and fat of your bipolar soul will never rescue you from the magical thinking you see in others. You know nothing, absolutely nothing of how excruciatingly cathartic good writing can be when authentically pursued, so rid yourself of that notion, too.

When This Poetry Deal Goes Down

when this poetry deal goes down so deep, you could
never return to that drivel you claimed was poetry, but
was merely contrived artifice— too afraid to feel the page
burning with conviction while you bounced around in
your micro-nadirs of depression; when this poetry deal
goes down so deep you hit a pay-dirt nerve with all the
brute strength of a freedom fighter reaching for a machete
to hack away at the boot on his neck, that ape-thing on
your back, or that n-word in the alley; when this poetry
deal goes down so deep, you hurl up to the heavens your
giddy dances of delight that you can hear the universe
laughing back its reply—*yes, that's it, baby!*
that is the Joseph you and I co-created and know!

when this poetry deal goes down do deep
no amount of sex will satisfy this wanton lust of love;
no friend-with-benefit in or out of bed could ever slake
the sultry sensuality of your solitude; let poetry render
and cleave your consciousness, let poetry be the final
abode that will take you in: that safe house you kept
breaking into but could never plunder or vandalize
because the madcap muses living there keep all kinds of
treasures and toys to distract you from the self-inflicted
terrors of day and night …

when this poetry deal goes down so deep
find the courage to take comfort in never leaving this
safe house, walk inside and with no malice aforethought,
simply welcome yourself home.

Summer Notes

as you sit and slowly rock on the front porch swing
listening to the momentous wisdom of thunder
and the prophetic catharsis of driving rain,
remember beauty

and when you hear the song of cicadas
ricochet among the trees, tired and heavy
under their blessed burden of green,
remember peace

creation's grace will make you giddy
when you bite into the ripe and reddest peach
and if you don't have a napkin
to catch the juice dripping from your chin
the universe will understand

watch the fireflies rise from cut and uncut lawns
to herald the sultry solitude of night,
and remember gratitude

        and I love watching you gaze at the birds
        scattering like jacks tossed from a child's
        sticky hand because you never cave in
        to that nameless fear that tried to invade
        our serenity here

because compassion thrives in summer
like lovers on their way home to make sweat and
babies under the humid moon while brooding
pigeons are cooing their approval in simmering
syncopation to the raucous roundelays of crickets

Palimpsest

Depriving ourselves of an hour's slumber, we spring
clocks forward, anticipating that first verdant and
luminous springtime evening, redolent of flowers and
potting soil, when a deep apricot sunset reluctantly
retreats like a fussy child to the necessity of bedtime.
The humming lullabies of streetlights crescendo then
diminish into the wispy and whispering white noise of
sleepy-time traffic. Some neighbor's radio roars the
Royals game ... a sauntering breeze teases your nose with
a little sweat, a lot of barbecued meat, while that first full
moon of springtime arcs up in grinning mischief,
looking for all the sky and world like a behemoth,
white-light period at the conclusion of some declaration
of delight. All big and supple, perhaps this lusty luscious
moon is the base of an exclamation point extended up
and out into the diminishing dusk.

Here on this hillside, funky with the impish odors
of infant grass and yesterday's rain, we watch the white
noise of exhaustion bounce off the worldwide wonder
of this gregarious Buddha-moon; we sit and wonder
about the sway-back ellipsis of that exclamation point,
allowing the summer-lazy wonder of tonight's
palimpsest to imprint us, connect us, this luscious
bright ball of infinity as it revels and rejoices
in the you-and-me light of this abundant Blessed Be!

Festival Kite in Night Sky

I.
Unlike the Dogstock Festival the summer before,
where the car got stuck in mud so malicious,
we had to pay a tow truck, it is raining — just enough
to piss us off as we break camp and pull up stakes,
and pack away the muddy implements and necessities
of our hedonism. You pause from packing and
between bong rips and sips of coffee, you survey the
detritus of pummeled tents, some still weakly halfway
standing in jagged misery. Curiosity peaks then
subsides as you count the upturned coolers with little
mounds of melting ice next to them, the abandoned
Mardi Gras beads half-covered in dog shit.

The music's long over now; its sweet vibrations
and the frolicking gyrations of bare feet are still,
but evident on the dewy grass and in the foggy brains
of the fretfully wakeful and even some of the noisily
employed, who load up trucks and schlep overused
porta-johns amid putt-putt golf cart engines drowning
out walkie-talkie banter, when suddenly it hits you;
there isn't enough acid or fungus in the hemisphere
to whisk you up and away from the sadness of leaving
Wakarusa.

As you drive back to the 9-to-5ness of your complicity
and complacency, you tell yourself with steely resolve
this joy-snatching, work-to-eat world won't blot out
the memory of how you sensed your breathing easy
when you were so psychedelic; you wanted to buy the
world a coke and turn it on with a smile all at once—
tripping balls the youngsters say. So many jams you
won't remember who was the best overall— good luck
this year, because everyone you saw really rocked
their sets. The work day world will not diminish that.
So easy to fall in love and lust at these things, but that
woman in the tie-dye dress in swirling greens and
oranges one can't find in nature made you look twice
as she smiled and you blushed because for once,
you were looking in her eyes and not at her cleavage,
and she tells you with her smile she appreciates that.
You mumble a pleasant greeting as you trip past her.
Confident in this newfound armor of memories and
music, you know the back-to-reality jolts might
succeed in the short term of maddening you,
saddening you, but Wakarusa was such big fun in
such short time, you toss your head back in laughter
and crank the a.c. and Widespread Panic bootleg and
hit the gas.

II.
The night before, I lingered by the Revival Tent,
foraging for any memory that still will fade over time.
Lonely, melancholy goosebumps made me fold my arms
against the mountain chill. Finding nothing and every
thing at once, I headed back to camp, head down,
distracting my letdown by hoping for some cool
ground score— maybe a twenty. Between my ears and
rib cage, so much sensory overload, so much energy
washes over me, I looked up in time to see a salt-and-
pepper bearded bearish man amble past, his t-shirt
reading THE HIPPIES WERE RIGHT in big, black
letters. I shook my head and laughed my cynical
approval to his receding back, continuing his way out
of my sphere of being, grateful for that respite from
the inevitable.

These crazy photographs, taken by technology,
preserved in memory, captured in the hula-hooping waves,
the undulating-jumping-dancing shouts to soul-dancing
riffs of music will be deposited in that little clutch of
consciousness; these moments define and buttress me.

But what I will always remember of Wakarusa was
looking up one night to see a kite ascend in vain to the
proscenium of stars, struggling to break free from the
gossamer string keeping it earthbound. Watching the kite
bob and jockey and buck and wing to the euphoric dance
of music, wind and rhythm below it, beside it the kite
twisted up and down in the increasing indigo of night,

sometimes barely visible in its moon-quest,
except for that eerie tail of glow-sticks and Christmas
lights waving wistfully to us below who are caught up in
the music and merriment of that last night of Wakarusa,
and as I give myself over to my body's need for sleep,
I am quite certain that the moon approves.

Watching TV with Grandma

Come back to a time worth remembering the television
commercial for a resort in southern Missouri says, and
my childish, innocent self is enticed, seduced by the
fiddling, the quilt-making, and the Shepherd of the Hills,
and that bounty of delicious looking food until my
grandma rudely awakens me about this era:
> the poison power of the word *nigger,* the noose
> and the white see that whorified our women,
> mongrelized our race; other atrocities
> spill out in a slate gray voice
> that matches her hair.

This commercial ends and another comes on
showing all these children — black, white and yellow
gleefully dancing and jumping around
a youthful white woman holding a plate of cookies,
and the children are singing
Tastes great like my mom's does!

Grandma stands up, shuts the television off with a huff
that hides the tears and goes into the kitchen to make
dinner. Amid the clatter of pots and pans I hear her
humming in a rich and robust grandmotherly alto,
Sometimes I feel like a motherless child.
I sit and stare at the black screen
and with a tear in my eye, I hum along.

A Murder in Volker Park (Springtime Horror)

Once while walking outside in winter's desperate
dying breaths and delighting in its fluttery futility,
the sudden flapping screech of so many blackbirds
slashing and swooping in wind-bare trees
wrested all relief of imminent spring from me —
feathery strands of terror that come with complete
self-knowledge. These black-winged harbingers of
winter mock late March sun with their psychotic
keening and fluttering fury, black spikes in trees
and sky, they herald the steadfast white malaise
where children dream of fatness
while their parents dream of escape.

Along Highway 45 towards Atchison, Kansas

1.
dark naked trees extend their branches in supplication
towards crisp january sun refracting light
of snow brightness that quietly embellished
these roughly hewn hills last night.
stubborn april blue sky foreshadows the battle-cycle
of winter into spring.

bean lake is held captive by a fragile sheet of ice
that conceals this lake's earthy murkiness,
and chokes the masses of reeds on its shore,
golden, mangled and jagged in their death,
bordering the highway east and west,
a tableau of elegant northeastern Kansas austerity.

look at these hills gloat over the aging state of railroads!
with no aspirations to mountainhood, each little gulch
and exposed root of big dead trees can bend the wind into
that stark melody the men and women who call this
home unconsciously hum way down in their beings as
they go about their days

listen to the silence as these Atchison hills gently mock
the shocks of corn that led brief but fruitful lives as they
sway to that simple, rugged tune; dusk ascends into starlit
night, winter's playful breezes departs with the sunlight,
leaving these shocks of the harvest staunchly standing,
gazing in gossipy contempt of the Iatan power plant
with its static man-made muscles.

2.
sunset splintered crispy and crimson into bare branches
and then, a cold silence shrouds the sky and falls,
waxes white, then sleeps. These highways and by-ways
are scars from human whips on the backs of these
simple Atchison hills, but when these lacerations of
transit heal, the roads will crack and recede,
        along with the echoes of tractors and trains,
the strains of tears and peels of laughter
will soon be nothing but a glimmer on this mighty
landlocked sea that must endure humanity's presence
to win their victory.

The Cleansing

The humid, heavy air in her bedroom
rises from their uncoiled bodies like vapor
from a dormant pond in summer.
Her suitor, intoxicated with the odor,
sighs at the ceiling, clutches a pillow
and falls fast asleep in their sweat.

His body sputtered and gurgled when racked and
consumed by the pain and pursuit of pleasure she
believed came from a mutuality that would wash
over them both now. But afterward, he shrunk into
nothing— a man without form and void …

She waits for any signal that
what she gave so unselfishly lives in his heart,
a fertile field yearning for more downpour,
but he snores the notion away, with eyes half open.

With the grace of fog rising up to vanish in that new
morning sun, soundlessly she slips out of bed,
sobbing silently as she pads her way to the bathroom
to rinse the copulation from her body,
his presence from her spirit.
Water mingles with tears,
streaming, clinging, caressing,
finally enfolding her to renew and protect
her self-love while her left big toe methodically probes
the awaiting emptiness of the thirsty, dark drain.

Summer Magic

All along the circumference of this swirling curl of
lonesome, the evening's humidity colludes with fireflies
alighting on my aching aliveness. I swat idly at a
wandering moth of some kind with my right hand.
My left hand is clenched, fist-tight, as if holding a Cracker
Jack prize, but I am holding nothing but *ennui* and desire.
Denny Matthews narrates another Royals abysmal loss,
while I contemplate the word *evening:* that is, a balancing,
a leveling. Slowly, a nascent indigo shifts the equilibrium
of twilight into night, its patient silence broken by the
giddy laughter of a skateboarding kid speeding under the
brightening beams of the streetlight across the street
and just to the left of our front porch, which is dark.
A night that yearns for hammock laziness, and I am
sitting, pensively, like coils on a discarded bed frame.

But then, I sense the silent swing of our screen door
opening as Lulu sneaks out in bare feet. I turn too late to
prevent the ice cube sliding down the back of my tank top.
Her giggles thwart the silence of my solitude.
Wet, and welcome in its dripping cold surprise,
I unclench my fist to swat away her other hands,
formed in the puckish claw of trying to tickle me.
I stand up from our front porch steps, pulling her to me
with a desperation I no longer conceal when I am around her.
Silently, I dare to laugh that laugh again, so I can halt it in her
throat with the kind of kiss that Summer double-dog dares

lovers give one another. Heatwaves give
way and rise to the stars adding luster to night's
canopy of sky: deepening, reveling, welcoming.

Whatcha thinkin' 'bout? Lulu asks, clasping her hands
underneath my tank top, not minding the perspiration
on me while I sit brooding. We begin this subtle sway,
invisible to anyone who'd see us. I say nothing for
almost a minute, content to rest my chin on her head,
before I say,

*Not a damn thing, babe. Just lettin' summer work its magic,
just lettin' the summer work its magic.*

Semester's End

1.
the pounding pressure of pursuing passing grades
erupts into the ecstasy of ended exams.
celebrations abound around the keggars and bonfires,
warmest wishes to keep in touch and to get a job
faithfully, foolishly fill the night air; drunken toasts are
drooled and hiccuped to the energy and ideals of youth,
complete with slurred speeches and sentimental sobbing.
thanks to the convenience of cliques, people not
liked and thus deemed unworthy to acknowledge,
much less speak to, can now belong for a temporary
while — we may even refill their cups with beer as we
talk together ... finally. we'll even grasp each other arm
in arm, yelling the lyrics to the school's fight song in an
atonal, exuberantly youthful with hopeful yearning;
but come the next day, with the bonfires extinguished,
we'll go back to our damned, despised distances,
hungover and afraid of the advent of commitments and
responsibilities of the impending commencement.

2.
rooms are torn down and packed into boxes and
milk crates; posters are rolled into their tubular
whiteness, stereos are stifled and stocked away,
and the school year's most played and much loved
music hides away in headphones and earbuds,
while the efficient dissonance of vacuums loudly

suck up soda pop and coffee, and other libation a
little bit stronger — vacuums that choke and sputter
at bottle caps, beer can tops, pennies and the shriveled
latex of used condoms … vicious vacuums that amplify
the isolation of missed goodbyes, drooping station
wagons, bloated SUVs and pickup trucks and truculent
trailers that contain the stuff of our rooms.

3.
we move like humming, hungry vacuums from one rug
to the next, sucking up substances essential for
sustenance; we choke and sputter at those heavy little
things hard to swallow. we move from room to room,
until we find that room within ourselves
at semester's end.

john wayne in the ghetto

when john wayne rode so tall in the saddle
in the little black and white box later clouded by color,
we didn't cringe in awe or fear

we hissed our outrage

daddy would snap the newspaper
and without even looking up
turn that stuff off son and sit back from that television

john wayne doing the cowboy thing
could actually make mama pop her chewing gum
in disgust, and when she rolled her eye that one
certain way …? hell even the marlboro man couldn't
mess with that!

mama and daddy knew the little black and white box
transmitted hidden deceptions meant to destroy little
black boys, such as a white man like john wayne
being proud of his plunder and prejudice

john wayne, oh so tall in the saddle
in the colored cube of illusion
didn't make me proud to be an american
and i damn sure didn't want to be no cowboy

i just wanted to kick john wayne's racist ass;
he made jeering a *chinaman* or killing an *injun* so cool
by simply riding off into the technicolor sunset,
so macho and chic, with that rugged *je ne sai qua*
that made hate as fashionable as alcoholism and
emphysema

oh yeah, hollywood put john wayne in the little black
and white box, made him ride oh so tall in the saddle
that he made us laugh laugh laugh here in the ghetto
while other folk somewheres else
laughed every bit as hard at amos and andy

The Prodigal Nerd Returns

        Oh, no, mothafuckas ... ten thousand times, no!
Don't go killin' fatted calves or cleanin' chitlins,
spare me on them spare ribs, keep them collards in the
kitchen sink; keep it movin' with that mac and cheese!
        NO NO NO ...

Y'all kicked me down, then kicked me out of my
soul-house, my palace of stumbling-but-still-striving
individuality, MY one's own One Zone of Presence,
of Is-ness! Kicked me so mean for so damn long,
Thelonius and Miles had to rescue me, had to whisper
through their music, *Play all the goddamn parallel*
fifths you want, fool, and quit worryin' about
        those other folk!
Y'all kicked, bullied and ridiculed me with YOUR
internalized homophobia, YOUR internalized ethnic
shame and animus for so lifetime long, Al Jarreau had
to teach me how to sing my own soft black song again!
And hell to the yes, Joni Mitchell and Janis Ian
saved
my
life!
The immortal Mbembe Milton Smith had to intervene
and rescue me from my very own festering and florid
poetry! So, keep your rejoicing repasts of salty soul food
for some other hapless exile, some other tacky-ass
prodigal brotha that will be bamboozled by such a
banquet.

I'd just vomit all that up on those Sunday *crowns*
and Akademiks gear made in sweatshops
and wouldn't care if it meant breathin' my last!
I rebuke your miserably myopic view of blackness!
I reject your Hotep heresies!

I came back home because I belong here! This is MY
soul-house! I came home because getting' on your
LAST black nerve brings more joy

    than a winning Pick-4 ticket, more devilish
and delicious merriment
than watchin' a sometimin' brotha fall and bust his ass
while tryin' to make the light
because his jeans were saggin' way too low!

                  And for the love of your
alabaster, appropriated *Jesus,* PLEASE stop cluttering
the air with your constantly clucking, *He done forgot
where he came from!* No, I remember well. I was the
skinny, goofy kid on the corner of 40th and Garfield
whose kitten you burned and left on my parents' front
porch, so that when you tried to teach me to defend myself
from your bullying, I would lash out in rages that would
baffle and scare my parents and siblings! And I admit
this white-hot elixir of rage would cost me much and
cost me many, but it gave me the only power I had to get
back what you stole from me! I remember all too well
where I came from — y'all cast out this outcast ...

    kicked my skinny ass WAY the fuck out, WAY
the fuck down so you could steal from me

something y'all felt a little too entitled to take!
How triflin'! How GHETTO!

And I admit that I have created too many impotent
spectacles, but I am much too old to be livin' outside
my own soul-house, my one's own One Zone, looking
inside like some besotted, homeless buffoon subsisting
on your meager scraps of dysfunction and duplicity!
I've masqueraded for y'all.
I've stepped-and-fetched for y'all.
I've charaded and paraded for y'all.
I've shucked and jived for your approval,
a hyper-sensitive exile
      leeching off the feeble gossip of your betrayals
and impending downfall!

I straight-up hate that poetry must be revolutionary
now! I can't keep up! I cannot abide the fact that
poetry must be charismatic and progressive enough
to keep a poet's ass ALIVE, never mind that ephemeral
jive called relevance!
      Oh ... and how now this little tar baby trap, this
little Pandora's box,
this *blacker than thou* monolith handed down to you
by those great white fathers of manifest destiny?
You all tried to make me choose between the uncle tom
and the street thug? PLEASE! I just kept it movin' past
that binary minstrel show; their seductions were
enticing, I confess.

But all of this naming, all of this blaming and shaming,
this self-nullification and defaming, with its insipid and
intractable hierarchies of disallowing and claiming,
leaves me more bemused than bereft.
In your collective slave mentality you called into question
my authentic black self and that is what you stole from me!
That is your unforgivable theft!

So, even though I was gone so far for so long that the
City Union Mission looked, smelled and felt like home,
I've done cobbled together somethin'
a little bass-playin' enough,
a little skinny enough,
a little queer enough,
a little Birkenstock and tie-dye wearin' enough to work
your LAST black nerve! Your sorry asses and your
projected madness will never break me! J.D.,
that Wayward Raven and Prodigal Nerd done come on
home, e'er'buddy, bringin' with me from my
self-imposed exile my best weapons
of poise and poetry, of writin' and SINGING
(not *sangin'* — y'all disallowed me THAT, too,
remember?)

I KNOW me now for who and what I am,
and I know you for what you is and ain't,
and now I know what you done stole from me!
I had these gifts with me all along, so ...

        ALL you niggas gotta BOUNCE ... NOW ...

Dancing Alone at the Edge of the Universe

So many times in so many ways I will saddle myself
with the pettiness of evil. And when looking for shelter
from that venial or mortal burden of evil exhausts me,
and I manage to look past the hypocrisies, betrayals
and dogmas of belief, disbelief and unbelief I have
wastefully stretched my reality into, I am dancing alone
at the edge of the universe.

      A dance of exhilaration and healing, I kick up
cosmic dust and asteroids while laughing loudly in the
newly known umbra of Pluto. Such moments come in
the burst of a milkweed pod, the wind blowing on my
bare feet in bed, even in the tiresome toil of busing
tables — even then, this dance is very lucid, very real,
transcending the tedium by leaps and bounds.

There must be a glint of malice in an atheist,
who, while rejecting the notion of someone or
something bigger than our absurd and bumbling selves,
still recognizes that inextinguishable spark of
greed and licentiousness, and gathering humanity into
mindless, dictated herds. And the cosmos only knows
how many righteous tongues of fire —

      apparently ignited by brimstone — replicate in
a mind replete with the Pharisees' religiosity: twisted
deeds and atrocities done in the name of god, who
seems to require two-thirds majority to pave that
well-intentioned road to paradise.

Astronomical in their extreme success, *isms* of both
ilks simply want to engulf the universe in that gaping
gyre that first frightened poor falcons and desert birds.

But somewhere that farthest star we take in with our
beady little eyes IS a source, un-stratified,
un-annihilated by dictums of dogma. And once we've
hacked ourselves and that farthest star into the bite-sized
oblivion we were craving, perhaps that source will try
and swallow us, only to belch and spew all prime
matter and back into the very cosmos of pure
potentiality we cringed from in the beginning.

But until that time comes, I content myself with
dancing alone at the edge of the universe.

Thinking about the Female Shapeshifter in STAR TREK: DEEP SPACE NINE (or, Your Amerikkkan Fetish)

The statue of liberty must be re-cast into the ghastly image of an infected Female Shapeshifter in DEEP SPACE NINE— heartless in her simple, cruel face — soulless in changeling cruelty, ruthless to her poor huddled masses. Warmongering shapeshifter, she emodies all that is industrial civilization

      and she will strip the stars from that giant blindfold called a flag and change them into swatstikas and burning crosses while coldly humming
    of thee I sing ... because
as desperately as opiates and oil,
the Nigger is Necessary in Amerikkka: from 1600 Pennsylvania Avenue to the trailer parks just east of long abandoned drive-ins where they suck down Fox News like cold cheap beer and fiends on the WWE,

the Nigger
is Necessary, and shan't be exterminated ... not yet, anyway ...

of thee I sing………..

The Nigger is Necessary,
as Cunt is Compulsory,

as Faggot is ... depends on one's mood and how the
flag can be fashioned into cock rings to torture,
maim, rape and murder — penises into bayonets,
machetes or billy clubs blunt, lethal traumatizing in
Police Room 619s all over Amerikkka ...
whatever passes for truth in advertising, that is,
truthiness in propaganda, the Female Shapeshifter
will teach us, just like Joni sings, that SEX KILLS
and permits the Compulsory Cunt, the Fiduciary
Faggot and the Necessary Nigger to enslave us into
hierarchies.

And while we tear down Lady Liberty and erect the
Female Shapeshifter, with her rapacious need for
order and her badly formed nose, this villain who
makes the Borg Queen look like a misguided Joan
of Arcadia,

I'm gon' say it plain,
you spewed your jism into a nigger wench and sold
your bastard child for profit ... so the Nigger was / is
Necessary – your Amerikkkan fetish
it is of thee I sing ...
just how long did you think you could keep your
petite digit on the trigger on the very notion of the
Necessary Nigger, of Compulsory Cunt and Feduciary
Faggot, on the very notion of humitarian intervention
and inclusive capitalism and not expect some
pushback, some non-magical gasp of resistance
before your Doc Martens stomp brains, your nooses
snap necks?

Amerikkkan greatness rests on a fulcrum of fictions that killed faceless, nameless black and brown bodies just because ... a country built by and for little King Leopold wannabes and vapid little Eichmanns laying waste and giving stillbirth to a nation where
the Nigger is Necessary ... **of thee I sing ...**
Hell, even Susan B Anthony knew
The Nigger was Necessary for a room of one's own within the confines of her subjugation; there were privileges worth savoring. She even foreshadowed the necessity of keeping a white right arm ...

Liberty ain't nothing more than the freedom to kill niggers with impunity, like your daddies did.

> Land where my fathers died
> Land where the pederasts' pried open the black legs
> **... of thee I sing**

Do not Jan Brewer your bloody shapeshifting finger at me, Amerikkan Festishists! You cannot rationalize your Nigger is Necessary atrocities to me anymore, for it is clear we are, in fact, a nation of savages — so governed, and thus oppressed, distressed, repressed, that our compulsion for the Nigger, for the Cunt, for the Faggot, consumes us and your whiteness, your Amerikkkan Fetish, cannot save you.

You, too, are doomed.

So shall it be written.
So shall it be done.

Sonata in C: One Drunk's Response to this Post-9/11 World: Supplication and Dedication

Amy?! Amy, are you there?!
You report from this screaming planet's grotesques
silences to expose
    fear decked out in an idiotic, patriotic pageantry ...
Can you hear me? Can you help me? Perhaps if I place
my hand on the radio, I can channel this malignant
silence clamoring in my inebriated soul, and maybe,
just maybe, you can hear me, and help me prepare for
struggle, prepare for resistance.

        Inside of me and all around me, this
dispiriting cacophony, these unutterable strains of
agony do nothing to lurch me out of the embalming
calm that alcohol, with its foamy golden pall, has over me.

This is the silence of a man burying himself alive.

    Beneath the Silence, one too-small sound;
a writing and gnashing of bone and soul,
enough to drown out the song of Piedade,
enough to know I'm too far gone, been way too drunk
for far too long, to possess the Secret of Joy anymore ...
Alice? Toni? I cannot hear to be healed by Piedade's
melody, and Consolota's drowning in said travesty
and the guns of execution are aimed at Tashi; and I am
numb and drunk, zombielike, in the City Union Mission,
where gay people are the targets of discrimination and
derision.

So Amy, or any of you good women,
guide me out of up from this lethal silence and see
me through the visions coming in this ... this ...
ramble— *she-ro,* now Muse, do what you do as
you report to the world the terrors of Oppression's
silence, and let every brutal truth be revealed in my
calling out to you!

Consumption

I was CONSUMED!

    By the SUVs on blowout tires that trundle like tarantulas out of the cut-out, cardboard comfort of the antiseptic Stepford suburban sprawl! Bouncing, wobbling wagons of decadence and waste, carrying lachrymose latchkey schoolchildren to prefabricated cellblocks and straight-up dungeons of lower learning masquerading as schools, where they manufacture cheap labor and consent, waiting for Superman to kick every child's behind into a bland conformity so pin-striped and pompous pimps of greed and bloodshed can profit as they pummel history and her-story into a sordid Taker religion of freemarket folly!

CONSUMED!

    By a secret *oh fuck yeah!*
when several of these poor misfits of puberty, so bullied and belittled by the hideous mechanisms of cliquishness and bullying belched up their brutal revenge from Columbine, to Paducah, to Red Cloud, Minnesota, their dumbfounded detractors and defendants alike falling from the hail of bullets, or fleeing in abject terror from the very *monsters* they helped create, and then, enable ... Misfits who found Oblivion supple and promising, and thus preferable to another second of enduring another taunt, or fist, or insult, before they vaulted themselves into the void they exploded their classmates into,

all the while yelling into the terror of their collective
vacuum *So much for dreams of grandeur in THIS Circle
Game, muthafuckas!* And the bullets flew, and the bodies
fell, and the screams careened Who needs some Sky Daddy?

CONSUMED!
    By the dragging death of James Byrd!
Ask his family if terrorism isn't alive and well! Guilty of
owning his black skin, while being in the wrong place at
the wrong time, breathing while black was his only crime
and that nine-tiered sepulchre we absurdly call
The Supreme Court cannot and will not tell me
otherwise!
CONSUMED!
    By the malodorous mockery of the martyrdoms
of Matt Shepard and Sakia Gunn, ripped from their
lifetimes and loved ones in those lifetimes, by the
impromptu viciousness homophobic fear-mongering.
And I wept bitter, acrid tears for them in my own
clandestine closet, where that sinister narcotic, Safety,
sucks her teeth in sassy comfort, while Truth, which even
now, in this meandering poem, STILL shames the Devil;
Truth points an honest finger, all the while whispering at
me in the closet,

    there but for the grace of,

    there but for the grace ... I pound my
tear-soaked fists into my ever-weakening knees, for all of
the above people, all these people, all OUR people, all
GLBT people executed on the capricious whims
of these sadistic bastards of brutality! True Believers,

so full of righteous entitlement to atrocity that they will never ever stop and gaze into the malevolent visage of the real masters they serve!

CONSUMED!

By the flatulent, but seductive alchemy of all this tabloid tawdriness, this virtual television reality breeding isolation and invective! How can you waltz, how can you cha cha cha, or vote the Muslim socialist off the island? How do you sleep while the downtrodden in their cardboard boxes, or in the bus stops shudder and weep? I, too, may be consumed, but I am not resigned!

CONSUMED!

By quasi-liberal eunuchs who step and fetch in your consumptive chase of consumption like so many demented sambos to incriminate, emasculate, and intimidate with your self-serving goal to eliminate me and mine in your mutual lust for war and plunder with your conservative minstrels of war and mutual greed!

CONSUMED!

By Wise Use wonks wanting to proliferate profit so wantonly, any living thing on this planet of emerald blue and cobalt green, must have a bar code or a price tag on it, and is only for your private consumption and comfort!

CONSUMED!

      Ultra-conservative wastrels of waste and war, your eugenically corrupt consumption reckons any non-white living human soul to be non-worthy and worth destroying until exhaustion or total collapse ... the only thing black that you love is your ledgers and balanced sheets as you rabidly pursue your money-green mania tinged with penis envy, all for the glory of your Frankensteined Taker god!

CONSUMED! By my country's insatiably fascistic need for all to comply and conform, pledging allegiance to the flag with a surveillance microchip in the upper FAR RIGHT;
CONSUMED! By this sudden obsession with national security at the expense of substantive democracy,
CONSUMED! YOU!
Up there in your alabaster towers of tyranny with your torrent-spewing transmitters and ditto-heads!
And YOU! Out there in your fortress houses with no front porches, sucking in the conspiracies of international banking cabals and installments of *The Apprentice!*
And sweet mother of Judas Iscariot! you Tragic Trinity: Clarence, in your so-called Supreme Court of cul-de-sac cunning; Condoleeza, giiiirl! with sweetness and sass, you sure kept them dune-coons running!
And your surname serves you well and suits you!
Suits you to a T — T for torture!
T for treachery! Extraordinary rendition will rend the captives free! This is our project for this new American century!

Oh! and I haven't forgotten you Colin, heavy sigh, heavy
sigh for your complicity in the Great
Rambunctious Lie!

    Y'all three-step and fetch and acquiesce
for trickle down droplets of power's largesse!
Y'all-three step and fetch and okey-doke,
    ignoring the stench of corpses and smoke.
Riddle me this, you trifling three in your dubious grace,
are you the crusading credits to our race?
If so, then I will RESIST with my dying breath
the three of YOU representing the *talented tenth!*
Y'all three aided and abetted this bucket ride down to
mass extinction!

    Mmm h'mmm ... y'all surely did! Scandalous,
    but girlfriend sure can rag out!
    And she be rockin' them shoes! You hear me?!
        There is too much horror there and here,
        I cannot abide it! Tiny shards of dignity
        will not succumb to nor abide it!
I AM also consumed ... but I am ... not too resigned ...
Piquant waters, your polluted raging torrent, so flooded
and consumed am I by the depths of my consumption,
breathing itself turn repellent, abhorrent I MAY
    be consumed, but damn it! I'm NOT RESIGNED!
Their Jesus dies, then etherizes and along come the neo-
cons to jump into that gaping gap of time and substance
with strict and urgent moral compunction while
Hitlerian high priests and priestesses of high finance with
their pillaging and plundering, while farting and foaming
out news-speak, calmly rationalizing and advocating
planetary destruction.

Drill, baby, drill!
Kill 'em all! Kill! Kill!

Their unmitigated gumption in this unstoppable consumption triggers flashpoints in my hung over mind, an aching that yearns for endless slumber.

But I stake no claim to the vow of poverty ...
I leave that to the cloistered prelates of power and complicity, ecclesiastical pederasty with popish duplicity, giving benediction and sacrament over the slave trade, all the while preying on their sweet little rough trade under their priestly robes and violating thumbs the stink of confession sex and ashes comes ...

    But no, I stake no claim to the vow of poverty ...
Give me things, things and even more things!
I want my reality show with enough money to bribe moribund protesters and silence my underlings, while my book-cooking stealth gets me absolved by the public through snakebite pundits of the bait-and-switch free market fraternity!

        I stagger past overpriced pottery,
        determined to win the lottery,
        but all my delusional dreams of
        consumption show no remorse,
        nor do they give release; and so
        alcohol, that narcotic to reason and
        contemplation begins its cunning,
        piquant flooding of the mind and
        soul for MORE MORE MORE!

I need to excoriate this flicking, lashing rage.
I need to expunge its seething element.
I need to exhale and expel every useless component
that stalks and starts the stockpiling of resentment.
With the utilities off, the house now in foreclosure,
my sanity took flight for sanctuary, any attempt at
composure led to the shakes in my own little Garden
of Agony, the hops and barley tyranny, where the pain
is so intense it actually has a sound:
rotting flesh sloughing off the bone of a corpse.

      These pints, these kegs, these joints and bongs,
last night's trick that took me home, gave little release,
certainly gave no comfort, thus no relief; so I resign
myself to the nadir of this depraved consumption,
for I have consumed, and resigned.
I accept my resignation
and then ...

Catastrophes and Conflagrations

1.
Hungover, with my little bungalow with a basement in
foreclosure while maintaining at a dingy pizza chain, and
kicked out of a boyfriend's house for way too much
consumption of his weed, of his beer, of his sex,
I landed back in the old neighborhood, two doors down
from my foreclosed house, paying rent capriciously,
stoking the bonfire of addiction maliciously — one more
safe haven for further self-annihilation of consumption —
of that neighbor's food, his house, his beer that he kept
with cockroaches in the icebox. Grotesquely familiar,
this pattern here:

      of slaking the ache of coming out, to excoriate
the ache of a necessary divorce, to expunge the grief of
parents who died too soon, who died too close.

        I cruised the parks and bars for remorse
or revenge, whichever one drove the libido and explosive
rage, a part-time weekend busboy, hustling for tips for that
next binge, building that invisible, stalwart cage to keep
the coiling spiral of my addiction from revealing much
too much. I owned denial with that drunkard's entitlement,
with the usual slurred speech and surly temperament.
Remorse and rage swirled on and on; drink too much
booze, screw nameless dudes; the whirlpool spun faster
and faster: remorse, then shame, yeah, sure! One more
dart game: a vicious cycle of disaster. In this trembling
house of my belching soul spin the cobwebs of deceit
mixing with those tiny dust eddies of conceit. In this
foreclosed house, in this foreclosed soul, I take another
hit off the foreclosed bowl.

That morning,
my hangover disallowed me the comfort of my bed,
so I lounged on the couch, watching *Good Morning America,* when they cut in on a COMMERCIAL, no less.
Flight #11 veered off its designated course with predatory speed, screaming across the sunny morning northeastern sky with innocents on board, hostages to history. At 8:46 AM CDT, Flight #11 embeds itself into the North Tower of The World Trade Center, smoke gushing out, then upwards in bulbous, black antipathy, blowing in the gusting wind like sudden death, unforeseen, not foretold; thick with the explosive rage of a deed overdone and intentional. Speculation from the talking heads suggests serious pilot error, mechanical malfunction. Rattled witnesses call in and suggest something calculated, something sinister. Confusion and chatter careened in our heads with the clarity unique to later summer, while the world wakes up and watches.

Then, at 9:03 AM CDT
OH MY GOD! OH MY GOD! OH MY GOD!
In plain world view, we bellow out expletives and exclamations, as Flight #175 seals the fate of the passengers on board as it slams the South Tower, erupts into a fireball, a missile-bomb of singular devastation. In the ghoulish colors of flashing orange and festering black and gray it is instantly clear that NOTHING on this mid-September day, NOTHING has been accidental.

Under the thumping pain of hangover, as I wiped away the tears that fell on the funk of my restaurant uniform, I grabbed that gossamer thread of fear tightening itself around the collective unconscious.

                    Microcosm of individual soul mirrors
the macrocosm of this visceral horror. So many
dismembered, so many dead in all that fire, so much fire.
We now learn with stark immediacy the *faithfully
departed* do not speak in tongues. Events of this day of
carnage and calamity get wrapped in the flag for the
sake of vengeance, for the sake of *retribution,* for the
sake of profit: metal ribbons on cars, with jingoistic
songs blasting out of them: simplistic answers
            to the simplistic question; WHY do they hate us?
Callous, collateral damage— 2,752 souls sacrificed for
power in this contest of contempt between Crucifix and
Crescent ...
                    ... meanwhile, in my own powerlessness,
in the depths of my drinking, I made sense of two things;
metal ribbons with insipid slogans on them cannot be
eaten, and that I can't even resist the yearning thirsts of
my darker self, MUCH less the dark designs of these
perpetrators of impending perpetual war!

2

The lights down at the City Union Mission burn with the
sadness, illuminate the funk and falter of men too long
gone; I took my sullen, prideful place among them ...
faceless, hopeless, something you scurry from in the
street, redolent of a desperation of circumstance that
I created.
                      A certain too-goddamned-early
October morning, I walked out into the Mission's
courtyard, fenced in to the West on Troost, with that
staid, dour brick wall to the East and whispered to myself,
Like father, like son.

into a drizzle not cold enough, passively heaving-
breathing, drooping under that blue-black darkness
not dark enough; Later that month, on October 28,
I refused the advances of a potential trick; in that
instant, my desire for slow and liquid suicide was lifted,
removed like so much funk and sadness left behind in
the Mission's shower. A cold drizzle swirled in the wind
and neon around me as I made my way down to the
Mission, drizzle accelerating, then descending into rain,
brisk and brittle cold, yet somehow strangely soothing,
as I waited on the last taxicab of the night to take me
back to the Mission, where my father found refuge from
his own depression, his own madness.

3

WHY should there be any discipline or restraint in this
poem? WHY should there be any *comprehension* in my
articulate voice when you show no restraint in your
rapacious torment and torture of the poor? So drunk on
your predator drones and missiles, you rabidly applaud
your caricature Christ marching ever onward and
onward to Zion, while raping Mecca and Medina —
all for the sake of Rapture and doomsday revelation!
This kind of Jesus is SO good for the free market, you
cluck to your cronies and cohorts, while death dances
and cavorts and entertainment distorts the reality of
what you're undoing!
You want conformity — I will resist!
You want compliance — I will resist!
You want restraint and *austerity* while you wallow in
denial! You simply do too much work to obfuscate the
truth behind the Big Lie!

Disproving, denying, and the whole time, depriving
the rest of some of their crust of bread; You mangle and
contort the truth for malicious aims, arming your
sycophants, fanning the flames ... so, go and build
your ovens, build your lethal war toys. Build! Build
with that *onward christian soldiers* zeal, go build
more prisons! For the rest of us know in all of your
brutal and beastly work, in all of that naked power
run amok, now gone berserk, we can and WILL
RESIST you at EVERY turn!

You cannot extinguish the truth of what you've done
and what you want to do! Even the dead that precede us
mock you, while this slowly depleted planet scorns you!
There is no bar code on the Truth of your homicidal
greed! Fools! Our songs of victory will daisy-cut the lies
from your tongue! Go! Go now! Your Aryan Almighty
is calling! We'll be waiting and ready for the struggles
ahead; we stand unbowed by the contagion of your fear,
we stand resistant while you slime and crawl to your
free-trade apocalypse! Equip your minions with that
M-16, deploy ten thousand other farces,
for in your impotent potency,
comes the strength and song of our Catharsis!
Catharsis Song (Rise Up!)

... now, quickly, Tashi, with your trusting heart,
your transcendent scar,
go to that place where our foremothers are.
Gather all those women, so torn by war.
Gather these men, so ripped by war.
We need a new song:

insistent and persistent:
a song of joy, sweet with the victory of peace,
a song resounding and resistant.

Piedade, 'neath the ocean's crest
your stifled melody clutched in your breast,
choked to silence by our vice
you'll sing again of Paradise,
with Consolota at your side.
Both of you re-teaching us how to abide
in work, in rest, and with each other,
our song of renewal, sister to brother ...

> *At every turn we will resist*
> *Revolt and fight again*
> *This Babylon, this Jericho*
> *This rude Leviathan*

This dissonant contradiction of perpetual war for perpetual peace, with its contradictions and crescendos booming ever loudly, must be excoriated from the consciousness! This apocalyptic blood lust must be expunged from our spirit, so that the healing song of resistance can exalt all who suffer and die under the grim tyranny of greed!

    How can we sing on this bereft and battered planet? When down through her-story and history,
nobody took the time to notice the fifth rider, with all deliberate speed, this regal woman on her thundering steed — *There is a fifth horse!*
> *Look up to the hills! Look! Do you see?*
> *Is it Yaa Asantawa? Is it Thraso Antimache?*

And while this woman rides, the sky thunders down its
grace, raining down its waters of uprising on every
parched tongue, on every bruised or battered face.
So, rise up, Jean Louise Jefferies Davis, rise up!
It's time to chant and channel down this Babylon.
Good late mother, hear this plea from your drunkard
son rise up, rise up, Sakia Gunn, chant and channel
truth to the power of your murder, and keep on rising.
Cindy Sheehan, channel and chant and hold them fast,
hold them accountable!

> *At every turn we will resist*
> *Revolt and fight again*
> *This Babylon, this Jericho*
> *This rude Leviathan*

Rise up, Piedade, it's time, the fifth horsewoman comes!
Allah Akbar, *peace be upon her*; Rise up, Tashi ...
transform the ghastly scar of your taboo to well-
deserved bliss, for here comes the fifth rider on a
ruddy-rose horse, exult and clamor for her kiss!
Allah Akbar, *peace be upon her*; Rise up, women and
womyn, rise up; every Kosovar dead, Allah Akbar,
peace be upon them ... from Chiapas to Selma
... from Sudan to Treblinka, rise up against all those in
power who KNOW the truth! Rise up, all you victims
against these greed-mongers, theses warmongers,
these blood-lusting for business, these butchering few!
With their scimitars and swords, with the cross and the
crescent, with their guns and fighter jets, landmine the
loam, bomb the plowshares, and STILL cannot make
any of us slaves, because THERE ARE NO SLAVES HERE!

There are no enemy combatants! Rise up, Emmit Till ...
rise up ... Allah Akbar, *peace be upon him* rise up and
sing truth to power; help me chant and channel; help me,
help all of us, excoriate and expunge. Help us all inhale
and exhale redemption's song.

REDEMPTION is that fifth rider.
      Redemption rides to stem that wicked tide of
hatred's vile lust for death, and violence for power's sake.
All of you, let us rise up, and start to heal ourselves from
all these conflagrations and catastrophes. We are rising
up and turning back this scourge of greed, exposing,
then excoriating the artifice of this Slaughter-fest Destiny!

> *At every turn we will resist*
> *Revolt and fight again*
> *This Babylon, this Jericho*
> *This rude Leviathan*

While Redemption guides us from the chasm of our
isolation, every living soul starts crooning or chanting in
remembrance for all of our war-torn dead, their war-torn
dead, a redemption song so rife with healing, so cathartic
in its mercy, even the sun is dancing, and the moon is
laughing at the impotence of our enemies, who drop their
weapons of mass extinction to close their ears to the
majesty of our song, as if they could ever drown out the
shameful depth of their atrocities!
      So many dead, so many surviving,
all of us STILL resisting and all rise up ... All rise ... up
Allah Akbar;

      peace be upon us!

Closure

At the first peel of the Angelus, at the first beckoning
tones of the Islamic Call to Prayer, we sat cross-legged
and composed, our eyes resolutely closed in remorse
and contemplation, our breasts heaving and our spirits
grieving all these victims, living and dead, of our wars
and our greed:
                Hiroshima, Nagasaki, the Middle Passage,
     Phnom Pen, Chiapas, Kabul, Grenada, Baghdad,
Tienanmen Square, Jasper, Texas, Aceh,
Wounded Knee, the Philippines ... the self-inflicted
terror of September 11, its aftermath of permanent war
— suddenly, like the collective breath of the dead
singing, a wind rose up, comforting, warm, bracing ...
did you hear that? Did you feel that? Are we healed?
You there! Please ... did you get healed?

Then, on this new day of atonement and rapture,
at the first peel of the Angelus,
at the first reeling tones of the Islamic Call to Prayer,
at the first zeal of these newly found tears of joy shed at
the Wailing Wall, on this new day, in this new Jerusalem,
on this renewed and newly forgiving *terra firma*,
while the sun dances, and the tides and moon
rejoice and sigh;

Let there be imagination without tyranny.
Let there be creativity without malice.

In our toils and our labors, in our leisure and our rest,
let there be a singular human excellence without
perfection, and its strident need to control.
Compassion and mercy will serve as the bricks, and
reconciliation will make an excellent mortar, as we
build a bridge across this embattled and bellicose breach.
Let us find communion in a radical Justice,
a radical Freedom,
a radical Peace.

And so, in the pulse and pulchritude of morning,
we persevered on that human, sacred bridge,
and all of the singing spirits who preceded us
in genocides, famines or pogroms;
their music bathed our work in warmth and wonder.

On this new day of atonement and rapture, we need you!
And you! And yes, you, too, the meek and shy one!
You can lay the cornerstone ... you! Over there,
with your knowledge and insight, we shall need you.

We need you, too.
    For as surely as this poet knows Saint Francis heaped
heaven's blessings on that long-forsaken sow, I know
we cannot begin this work without you. So, let us begin;
    and let there be chants and hymns and incantations,
yes, let there be psalms and songs to fill the air!
Now, EVERYBODY!

Smirk

This necrotic novelty arises out of the sinews and bowels
of that singular past-time that makes amerikkka great:
the nigger hunt,
and I am their latest prey.

I am dead.

    But know this: I smirked before the bullet impacted
all those intersections of my life and elevated my Is-ness,
my what-was-black-me — for blue lives spatter
black lives across time and space, and I lost the nigger
lottery, ran out of time and place because wasn't no place
left to run.

All black pure potentiality raped, emasculated
and/or burned
and/or strung up, I smirked the victorious rage of Odysseus
burning the unrelenting white gaze of Polyphemus— all my
best black pure potentiality and prime matter martyred for
your mendacity, your demigod demagoguery.

I smirked the smirk of the newly grateful dead
who know their rotting flesh and bones will mingle
with the particulates and poisons to form the terror firmer
that will be a particle in Gaia's sweet revenge.

So be it, then,
my dead flesh sloughs off, giving succor and sustenance
to toxic tiny creatures tunneling and tunneling
into the soil of a planet that will slough off white
supremacy like boilin' chitlins slough off stink on new
years eve.

I smirked the smirk of a nigger-faggot
who never liked the cop in the Village People
but loved his grandfather, a former cop.

I smirked that uppity nigger smirk — that one your
daddies taught you to hate; you spat BEHIND me —
exactly five paces when I walked past a group of you,
yearning for the day when you can make amerikkka
great again by spitting ON me.

I smirked because now I am in a better place
to hear the mocking laughter of the stars
as we jeer our collective invective
at that tiny metallic mess you impaled on the moon!

Black Lives Matter

Black lives matter,
yet the very air we breathe, this wondrous flesh
we inhabit our ever-resilient presence in this vast,
recalcitrant land grab
called America is *casus belli.*

Black lives matter ... and have mattered since the Middle
Passage, the cruel efficiency of slave patrols, whips and
pistols, along with the salubrious pleasures of coon hunts
and lynchings after church.

American power, with its oligarchs and hegemons,
has always known Black lives matter when exercising
their allegedly god-given right to terrorize through
myriad blunt traumas, poll taxes, redlining
or that catchy buzzword, *austerity.*

So-called liberals slogan up the rallying cry
Speak truth to power!
Those in power already know the truth that Black lives
matter, especially when the time comes for
manufacturing *untermenschen* before exterminating
them in massacres for being *uppity.*

From Roger Taney to Ronald Reagan,
from Rush Limbaugh to Charles Koch and Prescott Bush,
these acolytes of the pathology that is white supremacy

know all too well Black lives matter in a most
profitable, if savage way ... because if Black lives did
not matter, all these mechanisms, structures and
policies would implode, the fleeting comforts and
elegancies accompanying white privilege
would explode into a billion shards of shrapnel,
leaving no white people at all ... just PEOPLE.
From Darren Wilson to Bull Connor, from Woodrow
Wilson praising BIRTH OF A NATION to the
bloviating flatulence of Fox News, Black lives matter
as a fetish —
much like a tar baby.

Why do you keep on wishing to be in the land of
cotton when you are already here?
From sea to shining sea, THIS is your country to
run amok in! THIS is YOUR country, where you kept
severed limbs and testicles as *tchatchkas,* as souvenirs
much like your plundering brethren looted the
pyramids or other indigenous artifacts hoarded into
museums as gaudy testaments to your supposed
civility. THIS IS YOUR COUNTRY! You brutalize
then rationalize the atrocity of being in fear for your
lives ... without so much as a scratch on you,
while a black young man's corpse burns for four hours
in the midsummer sun.

Elegant courtier of Manifest Destiny, perhaps,
but y'all really should have ignored Rudyard Kipling!

DO NOT blackmail us with that sallow, surly notion
of reparation. It will not absolve you in THIS,
your beloved country of Eurocentric memory and
Aryan promise, where, beneath the twinned alabaster
avarice of white supremacy and privilege, lurks a death
urge so abysmally psychotic and addictive, Edgar Allan
Poe couldn't stay sober long enough to grasp its depth,
its breadth, its menacing metamorphoses.

This is your country, where Black lives matter even more,
because this is NOT an indispensable nation,
you are NOT a chosen people,
you are NOT a royal priesthood.
How can a nation that gorged itself on genocide and
slavery ever be?

Brothers and Sisters of the African diaspora, we KNOW
Black lives matter
by our Refusal,
in our Resistance,
by our Rebellions, and
in our Revolt.
With the imminent threat of police gunning us down
one by one, we summon the collective Resilience
of those who steadfastly and miraculously kept chasing
that long arc of Justice in the universe,
to challenge and rise up against 400 years of terror
by fiat, of genocide for the literal and existential hell
and profit of it.

WE WILL TEAR DOWN THE MASTER'S HOUSE.
It is the only human and humane thing to do.
It doesn't matter what plowshares or swords we use.
We will take to the streets, we WILL riot if we must.
We will tear down the master's house, and subvert
any ideology that presumes the master to have such a
dubious title, seeking only Justice, NOT revenge.
For it is then, and only then, that the enslaved master
WILL learn BLACK LIVES MATTER.
They ALWAYS have.
They ALWAYS will.

Uhuru (freedom)

Thoughts in a Dark Alley

I watch plumes from my pipe rising past telephone wires,
vanishing in the too bright light of a moon
that winks at me behind swarthy clouds.

Winter blows winds of cold accusation,
headlights and taillights drive past
with all the subtlety of a hearse,
and I wonder about those tiny moments of terror,
felt on the sunniest of days,
when I fool myself and others that someone somewhere
healed me from my blindness, because when I laugh
these days it is at a sister's or brother's expense.
I wonder aloud if the smell of exhaust from the car
could ever cover up the *rigor mortis* of a life not fully lived
and sloughing off like an indigent's funky clothes before
he shits in the shower of the shelter he'll flop down in.

Suddenly, as the final plume of pipe smoke rises
and the still hot pipe is pocketed for warmth in this
Tacoma dreary-fog, I shiver, wondering if I just now
heard a splash of suicide somewhere
but kept it moving, ignoring some stranger's pain.

In the same evil chuckle of the early Winter gust
that drives me back inside to stifling safety,
I can faintly hear someone, somewhere laughing at me
and thus accusing me— insinuation crackling on the wind
before it collides and splinters away
with the not-quite-slamming of the basement door.

The Belly of a Single Tear

The belly of a single tear
Is formed from anguished eye
The creviced dam that is the soul
Now leaks a liquid sigh

Pain long denied, now crystal, now clear
Glistens bright with woe
And runs its course with fragile grace
No comfort to bestow

soft, boyish hands

soft, boyish hands manifest the monstrosity of murder,
posing with machetes and machine guns while their
minion serfs do the grunt work of slaughter and mayhem
in bloody, muddy *theaters*

soft, boyish hands of prevarication and privilege,
flip the pages of the balance sheet, sending thrills of
approval to the mendacious mastermind,
just like women to be ravage a la *American Psycho*

soft, boyish hands on hips as eyes, beady with greed
and shaded under a *safari* or *cowboy* hat survey the land
to be cleared of primitives, mud apes or infidels
soft, boyish hands seldom strangle directly,
supple claws on black or brown necks
soft, boyish hands rarely threw the lynching noose
over that sturdiest branch of that strange fruit tree;
no ... meticulously moneyed and manicured, soft, boyish
hands draft the redlining legislation, take away collective
bargaining and send drones to kill the wretched of the
earth with the smirking flourish of a fountain pen;
soft, boyish hands punctuate the air with propaganda,
tap their drivers on the shoulder to take them
to the safety of a heavily fortified mansion or a cave.

soft, boyish hands wrote the code of Hammurabi
soft, boyish hands - thy will be done, Kemosabe!

Ode of Calm Release

There is this Ode of Calm Release
after great duress —
the silence that trails a twister's wake
to calm the panicked stress.

That one-eyed, funneled and twisting Wrath
of Nature's mighty hand
Chose a brief, destructive path
Which ripped across the land

But now, this Ode of Calm Release
at once — soothing, reviving;
A tenacious and persisting Peace
that sings to our surviving.

Joseph Anthony Davis has lived most of his life in Kansas City, Mo, where he attended Bishop Hogan High School and went on to somehow con(vince) the monks and nuns and Benedictine College in Atchsion, Ks, to give him a B.A. in English. When not writing poetry, he tries his hand (and sometimes his voice) at music, with songwriting, composing, and the electric bass getting the most attention. He works for the Broadway District of MainCor, a *blue shirt* counterpart to the ubiquitous *red shirts* seen helping to make midtown Kansas City clean and inviting for residents and visitors alike. *Black Lives Matter and Other Poems* is his first attempt at *literary adulting*, and it shan't be his last.

This project was made possible, in part, by generous support from the Osage Arts Community.

Osage Arts Community provides temporary time, space and support for the creation of new artistic works in a retreat format, serving creative people of all kinds — visual artists, composers, poets, fiction and nonfiction writers. Located on a 152-acre farm in an isolated rural mountainside setting in Central Missouri and bordered by ¾ of a mile of the Gasconade River, OAC provides residencies to those working alone, as well as welcoming collaborative teams, offering living space and workspace in a country environment to emerging and mid-career artists. For more information, visit us at www.oac.com

Osage Arts Community

www.ingramcontent.com/pod-product-compliance
Lightning Source LLC
Chambersburg PA
CBHW021450080526
44588CB00009B/787